BUT ARE YOU MAKING ANY MONEY

SOLUTIONS TO OVERCOME INCOME PATH CHALLENGES

MARC SHAMUS

iMasterLife.com

Edited by:

Marc Shamus

Published by:

i Master Life Publishing

But Are You Making Any Money / Marc Shamus
ISBN-13: 978-1-945719-06-6

CONTENTS

Grandpa Jesse & I back in 1994 during a visit

Personal Message from Marc Shamus

I wrote this book because of a strong voice I have in my head which has been inspiring me my whole life. You see, I had a very strong male role model, my paternal grandfather, Jesse Reynold Shamus, who pushed me with his words from a very young age and encouraged me to strive for personal greatness.

Growing up, I saw the impact that the corporate game had on my father with their endless demands for his time, work ethic and ever increasing performance in order for him to maintain being a successful manager of a large fortune 100 company. The carrot kept being raised higher and further away from him as he worked diligently harder to provide a stable household for our family.

Throughout my life, I have been a keen observer and experiencer of many life situations and obstacles, including multitudes of diverse financial earning experiences. Whatever your life background, I possibly have had circumstances just like you. I have been frustrated that I was working really hard to create income, but for some reason, the money was not coming in the way I envisioned it should.

I was frustrated that other people around me seemed to have it all figured out. I saw plenty of them with big houses, and a seemingle endless supply of liquid cash to spend but had no clue how they accomplished this. For income, I have spend most of my years as an entrepreneur (including Network Marketing) and have picked up a handful of w2 employment jobs (part time, full time and even seasonal) to fill the financial gaps on sparse occasions.

Yes, some of those employment situations paid me minimum wage or below and got me further in debt and even more behind on bills. Even in my 3+ decades of pursuing commissionable sales, I have had my share of challenges where I couldn't close enough prospects in a given pay cycle; therefore money was scarce and it seemed that I barely crept forward to continue for another day, hoping to have a breakthrough day.

Going back in time, in my late teens through age 21, I went through the college system and experienced first hand how things worked there, especially because I was a stellar student and was friends with a few key administrative personnel of the college. I did a few internships as well, which I learned a lot from, yet felt beyond disappointed from the overall experiences I had with them.

When I originally moved to California, I created immediate cash via short term gigs while I was putting in my share of auditions for all the Hollywood cattle calls that drove lots of people but very few bell ringers. I got a few small roles and even met some really fascinating people, although none of that would ever translate financially into any memorable noteworthy returns.

I even received WIC government support for a little while when my first child was born. This was directly after a conventional business did not pan out. I felt embarrassed about getting that help, but the assistance really made a big difference. I'm sure some of you can relate. I was strong enough to get back on my feet after a few short months. I moved on, ceased the government support and got out of that struggle. I have always been proud of this.

Regardless of all these income paths I have gone through, none went by without some positive gains. I learned a plethora of lessons that are useful for my path to a better financial tomorrow and making all the money my family needs. For many years, I have been hearing my grandfather's famous words striking like a grandfather clock in my head.

I just knew it was time to put this in writing and pass forward some pearls of wisdom from my experiences. In the writing of **BUT ARE YOU MAKING ANY MONEY**, I have finally been able to give back, pay it forward and help others get a grasp on why they may be stuck in their financial situation too.

Why You Should Read This Book

As you read this book, be open minded to change. Be honest with yourself to where you are in your financial life right now and be willing to absorb ideas I discuss. They can be an impetus that may change your life in big ways.

We may have good intentions in life but things don't always turn out the way we plan them. My hope is to inspire you enough to plan ahead and consider things from a greater perspective.

Consider the welfare of you (if you are single) or your family (if you are married with kids) if tragedy should strike and cause you financial grief. Enduring with and dealing with a tragedy is bad enough, but not having the finances during that time is even worse.

This book will help you gain the knowledge of the challenges with certain income paths. It will give you some food for thought about those paths and some solutions to making that path turn financially to your favor.

It will then be up to you to take the necessary action steps to apply the concepts shared with you in this book, **BUT ARE YOU MAKING ANY MONEY.** You must put in the effort and engage in "Do" mode to create results.

Denial or Anger to my message will hinder you breaking through your own personal struggle. In order to walk the walk and achieve the results you desire, you must be willing to get out of your own way. Excuses, Fears, Procrastination and perfectionism have got to be removed from your habits and mindset.

You can take your life from ordinary to extraordinary with this new gained knowledge. What you do with it is truly up to you. I am rooting you on all the way as you read this book and start on the journey to the new amazing financially wealthy YOU!!

INTRODUCTION

Grandpa Jesse was a very serious man. He was not one to spend time clowning around. He would get right to the point without wavering in the wind with a confusing message. This is how he was in talking to me even from a very small age.

I remember so clearly how I would talk with him with excitement about something I was pursuing. More so, if it was income related, he would politely listen until I stopped talking. Then he would ask the same 2 questions every time.

1) How's it going?
2) Are You Making Any Money?

Being younger and also having the feeling that perhaps I was not living up to my potential, I would blabber on. I would make a lot noise, produce tons of wind telling my grandpa why I thought things were doing "ok" and how I had bright inspiring plans to make the future with that endeavor so incredible.

I never lied to my grandfather, yet being proud of my efforts, I just wouldn't always admit the full truth that things were not producing the results I wanted. Funny enough, he would also have the same rebuttal no matter what I said back or how colorful my story was. It is this famous line that till this day rings in my head. I hear his voice say over and over:

"But Are You Making Any Money?"

Yes, seeing a situation for what it really is… this can be hard to do. In my youth and pride, it felt easier to rationalize away and find excuses for why I was not seeing financial victory. This is a lesson in life I wish you learn faster than I did. Face the music and when things are not going according to plans, own up and be truthful to yourself.

Grandpa Jesse would see through my pride and repeat himself over and over by saying:

"But Are You Making Any Money?"

Much time has passed. Now I am a man in my 40's. Although my inspiration, friend, role model and grandpa is no longer alive, he lives on in his pursuit to get me to comprehend the fundamental financial lesson of being real about making money or not making money. You either are making money or you are not. You cannot be doing both.

Keep in mind that just because you have income coming in, it does not mean you are truly making money. It only means that you have begun your journey to produce income. Making money only begins when you can create a comfortable lifestyle through the money you earn. Grandpa Jesse defined making money as having more than enough to support a very comfortable lifestyle including money saved for retirement years.

My Grandpa retired from working in 1985 at the age of 67. He lived a very peaceful, relaxing and quite comfortable retirement with my grandmother for 22 more years until his death in 2007. Yes, he had social security and a pension from the "Blueprint" company he retired from, coming in every month. This provided a surety for continued income. However, he had multiple fold in personal savings what he ever received from those things during that same 22-year time frame.

If you were fired or left your income producing position today, how long could you go on before you get into financial problems? How long from now till your cell phone would be shut off, car repossessed, house foreclosed upon, end up in a divorce and find yourself having to live in a homeless shelter?

If you are like most people, the answer is less than 1 month. If your answer can honestly attach the label of "years" after the end of it, congratulations, you are "making money" according to Grandpa Jesse. I pray that you get to that level of financial success. You deserve it and you are worth it.

I will cover in this book what I define as the 12 income path games that you may face. Each has their own truths, challenges and solutions to overcome. By no means am I putting anyone down who is pursuing any of these paths, as I already outed myself as having gone through all 12 of these paths at some part of my financial life.

Without further ado, here we go…

DOWNLOAD YOUR GOAL SETTING GUIDE

Get access to your FREE goal setting guide by going to

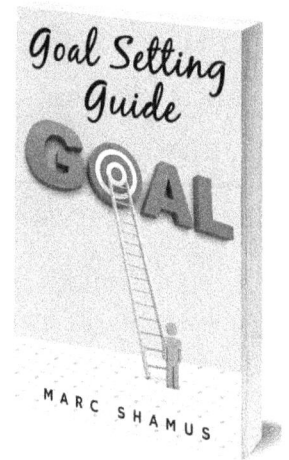

http://iMasterLife.com/GoalBonus

Inside the bonus guide, you'll discover...

• What are the **Building Blocks** of success

• How to set up **Success Planning** to reach goals

• Very powerful methods of **Implementing Success**

•10X your chances of reaching goals via **Success Management**

NOTE FROM THE PUBLISHER

i Master Life
EMPOWERING . ENGAGING . TRANSFORMING

Thank you for purchasing this **i Master Life Publishing** book. Our goal is to get high quality <u>Life</u> <u>Mastery</u> materials and other worthwhile media into the hands of incredible people like you.

FOLLOW US:

Join our mailing list and get updates on new releases, deals, bonus content and other great publications from **i Master Life Publishing**.

iMasterLife.com/fan

SUPPORT US:

If you enjoyed this or any of our other books, would you please help support **I Master Life**. The sustainable revenue you provide ensures we can continue to provide publishing the very best media possible for you.

Just go to this link: **iMasterLife.com/Fund**

Thank You!

Marc A. Shamus

    Founder

LIMITED INCOME

PATH

Summary

The quantity of money made from limited income path type of work may cover some of your basic bills or instead go toward entertainment. Usually, that is about it. It truly depends on how much your expenses are on a monthly basis. The more liabilities you have, the less impact a limited income type of job will have.

Don't expect to have a jet set lifestyle or anything too lavish for that matter. Limited income work is a great thing to pursue if it is just used to aid you with income while you pursue other work which will be financially worthwhile.

1. PART TIME GAME

Some people may choose to take on work that is only part time. Perhaps the job is only offering so many hours each week or the employee is choosing how many hours they wish to work. Either way, the hired person is happy to have this position and be employed for a small number of hours any given week.

The pros of this are obvious in that it allows for more personal time and flexibility for scheduling of life around the work. The part time employment choice is ideal perhaps for:

1) **College Students**

2) **Adult Students** pursuing professional certificates & licenses

3) People already with a **Full Time** job

4) **Entrepreneurs** who are looking for cash flow while building their dream enterprise.

5) **Senior Citizens**

The people in these situations feel that they need to focus on their primary goals at hand which is:

1) **College Students**: A college degree and job placement in the chosen field of study.

2) **Professional Adult Students**: A professional certification in the field of their choice (Insurance, Real Estate, etc.), professional license in same field and Agency or Practice acceptance to hang their certificate at and start working.

3) Full Time Job: Enough extra income to cover the gap in expenses from what money is coming in from their full time job.

4) Entrepreneurs: Enough extra income to cover the gap in expenses from what spendable revenue money is coming in from their business ventures.

5) Senior Citizens: Enough extra income to cover the gap in expenses from what money is coming in from retirement pensions, retirement accounts, social security, life insurance policies and support from family members.

It is a very good thing that these folks can achieve their intended goals and have the part time work to help them in the interim. For many who choose this, this seems to be a logical fit and solution to their needs.

BUT ARE YOU MAKING ANY MONEY

However, when we look at part time work from the view point of currently being in financial success, this attempt to leverage their personal finances seems to fall short for several reasons:

1) College Students:

Consider that College degrees take a lot of money, time and effort to successfully achieve. The more time spent away from studying, essays or other class learning can be detrimental towards degree completion. A student may receive lower grades or potentially fail in certain classes as their level of distraction goes up.

Also, if the student did not have scholarships or grants to attend college, they may have to pay their own way. This means the student may only be taking 12 credits per semester; thus they may take perhaps 3 years to graduate a junior college with an associate's degree and 5 years or longer to graduate a fully accredited 4-year university with a bachelor's degree.

Thus, how many hours every week can they work and how much money is a college student really earning if they are so busy with studying for schooling and the money they earn is paying their bills? This is even more frightening when we consider how many years they will be attending college to complete their degrees.

2) <u>Professional Adult Students</u>:

Consider that these professionals must enroll in certification classes either online where ever they have internet connection or at an accredited professional college. It can take anywhere from a few weeks to a few months to complete. Then, they must pay for and schedule a state exam in their chosen field. Only once passed, can they find an Agency or Practice, set up a contract and begin working.

There are some of these professionals that have challenges with passing the certification class and then there are definitely many who may have to take the state exam a few times to pass it. All of this adds more time and expenses.

Although the schools for the certifications and state exams are not terribly costly, people do not generally get scholarships or grants for this purpose. Therefore, unless the professional pre-arranges for the Agency or Practice they plan to contract with, to reimburse them later on for these fees, they may have to pay 100% of their own costs.

Thus, how many hours every week can be worked and how much money can a professional college student really be earning if they are so busy with preparing for certification classes and the mandatory state test for their chosen career?

3) <u>Full Time Job</u>:

Consider that these workers are busy enough holding down a full time employment elsewhere. Their part time job is almost always going to be secondary to their primary full time job. They will not choose to do anything to jeopardize that bread winning income. This means by default, there is a conflict created whereby certain demands or needs of the part time job may interfere with the employee's commitment to their full time work.

It stands to reason that they will not be able to work many hours at the part time job due to scheduling challenges. They also will not be able to move up the corporate ladder in those Part Time jobs since those positions are typically rewarded only to candidates working full time in their company. Therefore, earning substantial pay raises in this part time job become more challenging.

Thus, how many hours every week can be worked and how much money can a person already full time employed elsewhere really be earning?

4) **Entrepreneurs**:

Consider that entrepreneurs are busy enough getting their own business off the ground, not to mention exhausting all of their own money and resources. Their part time job is always going to take second priority to their dream idea becoming their full time income source. They will not walk away from that dream, so any high stress obstacles at the part time job will cause them to look for another part time job elsewhere.

It stands to reason that they will not prefer to work too many hours at the part time job due to the need to grow their own business. It takes a lot of time, money and effort to build up a business and if the entrepreneur is putting in too much time at a part time job, it becomes a catch 22, whereby they will have less time to devote to their own venture.

Many high paying jobs do not prefer people with little employment experience in that field (as requested on resumes) Many times, these employers' will show a bias against self-employed people who tend to be more free thinkers. Corporations are more preferential to employees they can control. Therefore, many entrepreneurs find themselves getting hired by workplaces that may start them at more entry level paid positions.

Thus, how many hours every week will the entrepreneur choose to devote to a part time job and how much money can they really be earning based on the circumstances?

5) <u>Senior Citizens</u>:

Seniors may not have to worry about the costs of raising young children, schooling expenses, state exams, pressure and time crunches of full time work, nor the challenges of running their own business. They have the luxury of more freedom to discern what work they choose.

The obvious challenges faced by seniors in the work environment include potential discrimination due to age, diminished strength to lift heavy items, certain health challenges that may limit their abilities as well as technology impairment which can impede them performance on certain electronic equipment.

Let's face it, many of these seniors are in the years of their life whereby they may mentally want to be retired, yet they are not able to, due to their lack of appropriate finances. If they had all the money they needed, they would not need to work and would pursue whatever hobbies and passions of interest they want.

Thus, how many hours every week can they physically work and how much money can a senior citizen really be earning if they are wanting to achieve a comfortable lifestyle or take a relaxing retirement at some point in the not so distant future?

CONCLUSION ON PART TIME JOBS

I do see how a part time job can fill the financial void for people. However, the only way it can work, in my opinion, is on a short term basis, since it is very clear that there are not enough hours worked to make any financial difference and the distraction factor is very high in all cases.

SOLUTIONS

1) College Students:

The college student would be better off taking the time to apply for grants and stipends. Also, they could work hard on their studies to get good grades so they could also apply for scholarships. There is a huge amount of untapped money that could be rewarded, if a college student wanted to put in the effort for it. This would alleviate their distraction of the part time job.

2) Professional Adult Students:

The professional adult student would be wise to secure an Agency or Practice contractual arrangement before going through the certification and state licensing. Many will offer to reimburse the costs of the schooling and licensing after completion (as long as the candidate does indeed contract with that Agency / Practice after securing their license).

They should also secure a small private or public loan to afford the costs attached with both their regular bills plus schooling and licensing costs. This will enable this person to have 100% distraction free focus on finishing quickly these requirements and start working vastly quicker. Then, they could be done with certification and licensing in just a few weeks propelling them to already be making money in their chosen professional field.

3) Full Time Job:

The truth is that the Full Time worker is attempting to hold on to a Full Time job that simply does not pay them enough. The part time job is their excuse to themselves that they are making a tiny bit extra. It is never enough money though as they sacrifice much of their extra free time to pursue this.

They would be smarter to face the music and in the time they are putting into a part time job, spend it instead seeking a higher paying Full Time job. Not only will they not be trapped in a perpetual state of feeling tired, they will also gain back many hours of personal time again.

4) Entrepreneurs:

Cash flow is king. To entrepreneurs, it can be the difference between having a thriving business and having none. They also will be living on the street if they do not have enough of it. So even though the entrepreneur may struggle with this, they are better off going after micro-loans through peer to peer crowdfunding type of platforms to raise additional capital for their business and life expenses. Entrepreneurs must resist the temptation of the part time game as it takes them away from their mission.

5) <u>Senior Citizens</u>:

Seniors also do not want to be stuck in the part time job long term or they will never realize a stress free retirement. Even if a particular senior enjoys their part time work, they may never create large income while pursuing it. The senior is better off taking full time work for a long period of time until they reach a point that they do not want to work any longer.

This way, they can accrue much more money than they ever could with just a part time job. 5 – 10 years of full time work while a senior is in their late 50's or early 60's can give them many more years of not having to work at all instead of having to work part time while they are in their 70's, 80's or even 90's. This is important since the older the senior is, the harder it is to find a job that will hire them.

There are also government and private assistance programs for seniors. These may also be a terrific fit instead of the Part Time job since the senior will have their time freedom to do whatever they want. Like all assistance programs, it is all about qualification, voluntary asking for the application and the senior submitting the application so they can get approved.

2. GIG SIDE PROJECT GAME

Some people do not want to commit to a part time nor full time employment as they really value their time flexibility. Getting Gigs seems to gel well with musicians, actors and entrepreneurs, especially since the pay most often is immediate (cash in lots of cases). It really allows the person to be proactive creating wanted funds while not filling up their schedule long term. This is super for being able to pay bills while pursuing their passion.

BUT ARE YOU MAKING ANY MONEY

The challenge with Gigs is that the work is either short term or unpredictable. If short term, it is not rare for the gigs to be just 1 day projects; at times just a few hours. Even if you are blessed to find a longer running Gig, as mentioned, the pay is nominal versus the traveling expenses attached to the Gig. If you need to buy supplies to satisfy the work needed for the Gig, you could exhaust all or part of the pay right away.

People that choose to work for Uber, Lyft, Sidecar and other contract independent ride share services are actually Gig Side Project workers. This is a great example of unpredictable Gig work with lots of expenses like gas, car maintenance, car repairs and much more. The folks who do this work love the independence they have, yet if one looks at what the average profits which a ride share person makes, it is not much more than an entry level job at best.

Thus, how much money can a person doing Gig work actually earn if it is so sporadic and/or not guaranteed long term? I know we both know the answer is very little, since the high majority of musicians and actors I ever met were starving, struggling entertainers who barely made ends meet each month.

And the entrepreneurs like myself who do Gigs fare no better, since the money you made from a small gig is spent before you can blink an eye. Entrepreneurs also seem to be a little fickler on what Gigs they are willing to pick up since some of them are looking for more of an entry level, employee minded person, not a free thinking decision maker.

CONCLUSION ON GIGS

I know from personal experience doing Gigs that one can bring in quick cash without waiting for a commission from a sale to clear or a company to give a pay check a few weeks later. As long as you are perfectly comprehending that a Gig is just that, short term money, you are good. Just never get into a delusional belief that a Gig can create long term financial stability and lifestyle.

SOLUTIONS

Gigs are good to get cold hard cash in your pocket today. If you need that money now, then securing a gig can be a good match for you. Conversely, since you will never make any decent long term money with a gig, you should make some other plans through a different income path which will help you achieve this. Only then will you make enough money to get your dreams.

3. TEMPORARY & SEASONAL GAME

Some people choose to pick up short term work assignments that are only meant to last for a limited period. This work may be assigned from a personnel job placement firm or direct hire. Either way, it can be a great way to secure additional income before big holidays or while you are in between full time permanent work.

BUT ARE YOU MAKING ANY MONEY

The challenge with Temporary & Seasonal jobs is that the work is short term. In fact, Temporary work comes with the hidden surprise of not always knowing how long the firm is going to employ you for. Seasonal work is notorious for only keeping you on payroll until right around the day of the big holiday.

Knowing that this type of work has a short span, creates a direct red flag that you will not produce huge long lasting money. You may produce enough to buy holiday gifts or keep you afloat until your next long term income choice comes along.

Thus, how much money can a person working Temporary & Seasonal jobs actually earn if it is so short lived and the work assignment could end abruptly at any time? Pretty obvious that it is not all that significant.

CONCLUSION ON TEMPORARY & SEASONAL JOBS

Every time I picked up one of these assignments, I knew from the start that I would only be needed for perhaps a few weeks or more. Similar to Gigs, be conscious that this is short term money. You will not break any records with the pay you receive from Temporary & Seasonal jobs.

Temporary and Season jobs are a great solution for many people's emergency expenses that come up. They are an excellent way for someone to raise money for things such as funeral costs, small medical bills, a small wedding or an unexpected car repair expense. Since there is no long term commitment, this job may last just long enough to raise the funds needed for whatever tiny need a person may have. Best part is the person did not have to go into debt with a credit card.

An example of gaining Seasonal Work was my choice to create some additional money for the Holiday season one year. I picked up work for Amazon at one of their distribution warehouses. The work was not difficult, yet very tiring due to the physical requirements of lifting heavy boxes and the long overtime hours. Overall, it was a great experience for the short 3 weeks it lasted. This Temporary assignment brought in additional cash to pay for all the holiday gifts. That was pretty sweet.

SOLUTIONS

In my opinion, I recommend to only pick up Temporary & Seasonal jobs if you are out of work beforehand, have an emergency or need to generate money for holiday gifts. Overall, if you can help it, it is best to avoid most Temporary & Seasonal jobs and aim to find a much more lucrative income vehicle.

4. WELFARE GAME

There can be very legitimate reasons why someone would receive government assistance. Many very talented people from all diverse backgrounds have used this type of support at some point in time. For those experiencing major struggles, the welfare programs can be a godsend to provide needed meals and supplies.

BUT ARE YOU MAKING ANY MONEY

The challenge with being on any of the assistance programs of welfare are that if you want to remain on benefit, you must remain qualified for such assistance. This includes the provision that states that as you pass certain personal income, the amount of financial support you can receive will be reduced. For certain people on welfare, this becomes a negative sticking point as they choose to not work much or at all so they keep receiving benefits.

The folks who start to become complacent with receiving the benefits start adapting a hand out mentality and their behavior elicits something on the grounds of both entitlement as well as stubborn unwillingness to produce income outside of the benefits of the welfare assistance programs. It doesn't take a genius to figure out that if you are not putting in any effort, yet are receiving benefits off the backs of others efforts, you are not going to make much money.

Thus, how much money can a person on welfare really be earning based on the circumstances of them either hardly working or not working at all? I know we both know the answer is very little, even if they "played" the system so they have a survivable amount of welfare assistance coming in every month. They will not be able to create any dynamic lifestyle including taking personal vacation trips and escape the mediocrity they exist through.

CONCLUSION ON WELFARE

I do see how receiving much needed assistance can help a person to either get back on their feet again or stay afloat. However, the only way it can work, in my opinion, is on a short term basis, since it is very clear that there is not enough financial support coming through to make one wealthy. Furthermore, the drain on the other citizens is tremendous if everyone just wants a handout and does not provide any value to society themselves.

SOLUTIONS

The welfare recipients should not just sit on their behind while receiving the benefits. They should be constantly proactive seeking to improve their situation by finding gainful employment of some kind or creating something of value that people are willing to pay for. Moreover, they should choose to be part of the solution and not part of the problem.

CAREER INCOME

PATH

Summary

The quantity of money made from career income path type of work may create some security to cover your basic monthly bills. It can also afford a person some extra comforts and fun entertainment. How much comfort and security you experience truly depends on how much your salary or earnings are on a monthly basis versus your expenses. The more liabilities you have, the less comfort you will have.

Where this type of income path falls short is freedom of your time, lack of leverage to produce substantial wealth during your working years and difficulty to prepare for a lush retirement. Career Income work will provide steady money every month making financial planning much easier. The key in this work is to stay with it long term and establish a good retirement account, like a 401k and life insurance, that you can access once you get to retirement years to supplement your social security check.

1. Minimum Wage Game

I know that the search to find work is sometimes riddled with a long process stemming from resume or cv (curriculum vitae) submissions to numerous companies followed by rigorous interviews with select management personnel. Some people feel the desperation to just be done with the process, throw up their hands and have a job already.

I comprehend this anxiousness since the person has spent perhaps far too long without employment or is really needing to have money to pay current bills that are due. Getting hired and being told that the starting pay will be right around minimum wage is not the money song most want to hear, but at the very least, they have found gainful employment.

I also realize that there are others who may have been able to secure work without much struggle at all, yet they too are faced with a mere pittance commensurate of minimum wage. This is the real life price of widely available entry level positions. It means that more new employees in a company will earn at the lower totem pole on the company payouts.

BUT ARE YOU MAKING ANY MONEY

The challenge with Minimum Wage jobs is that the work never brings in more money than a few hundred dollars a week, at best. I've never heard of anyone in all my years creating their dream lifestyle on minimum wage.

Thus, how much money can a person working Minimum Wage jobs actually earn? No rocket scientists needed here to figure this out.

CONCLUSION ON MINIMUM WAGE JOBS

Minimum Wage jobs are one of the biggest insults going on in the working world. The company hiring a person at Minimum Wage is saying that this person is good enough to perform needed tasks to grow the company, yet truly ONLY an entry number in their computer screen. Otherwise, please explain the company's lack of concern over monetary compensation for the hard work of Minimum Wage employees.

Grandpa Jesse always told me that a company choosing to pay you at the bottom of the barrel was a waste of your time. He said that you would be better off pushing harder to find other work even if it only paid an extra dollar or more than Minimum Wage. Grandpa said that you can tell a lot about both the management of a company as well as how much they value their employees directly based on how much pay they start their lowest paid employees at.

SOLUTIONS

Grandpa Jesse worked a good part of his older years in the blueprinting arena. Even though he was not the owner of that "Blueprint" company, the firm he worked for, the owner knew my grandpa was a master in both photography and business development. So in spite of the "owner's son" not wanting his father to give Grandpa

Jesse as much input controlling power as he did, the company rose to the top of their industry on the backbone decisions of my Grandpa.

Looking back now on the high level precision Grandpa had, it gives me chills. Realize that they had a few internal company problems. One of the most pressing was company morale. The employees would show up, work the least amount they needed to so they were not fired, and then leave when their shift was over. So many companies face this same emotionally detached issues with their employees, it seems.

Grandpa Jesse knew how to turn this situation around 180 degrees. So he told the owner of that "Blueprint" company to raise the Minimum Wage about 50% higher and also make the other salaries higher as well. At first, this idea was considered really radical. How would this make sense or even work? Did the company even want to have more expendables and cut into profits even deeper?

It took a small while for this idea to be accepted and implemented. To the amazement of the "owner's son" and a few of the department managers, the employees embraced this new policy and morale shot through the roof. Like a hot knife melting through butter, the company's production and reputation shot to all-time highs. The well paid employees started to take ownership over their work and stopped worrying about the clock.

This "Blueprint" company provided the best quality finished product at that time in the United States for that industry. Just so you have an idea how big they became. If you went to any Shopping Mall, Plaza or Office Building before 1985 (the year Grandpa Jesse retired) you would see the directory "You Are Here" signs all made by this #1 "blueprint" business that Grandpa Jesse spearheaded.

I know that you may not have control over affecting this type of change at a company you work for that offers minimum wage, yet when applied, this strategy of my grandfather, it always works. If you are faced with a company who is offering minimum wage, you are best off to work diligently to seek other employment.

Don't waste your precious time earning next to nothing. You know you can do better and now go after it. Don't just hang around hoping things will get better. Don't buy into the rhetoric that everyone started at Minimum Wage and worked their way up. In most cases, that is corporate lip service to keep you stuck on the merry go round.

2. COLLEGE DEGREE GAME

College is one of the most talked about conversations for secondary school children and their families. There is this big push for High School youth to perform well by getting good grades and/or performing as a top athlete in sports. They are expected to take their ACT or SAT standardized tests and score well on them. Then, there is the driving and flying all over the place for visitations to a slew of college campuses. This is followed by the race for securing scholarships, grants, stipends and loans.

Applications are submitted to all the top choice colleges of that student. Oh the joy…the waiting game begins as the anticipation builds. What school is going to accept the student? Will it be the College of their choice? After a few months, acceptance and denial letters start to slowly trickle in. Then, the day comes when the final decision will be made on what school the student will attend. Everyone is excited and the student is getting ready to become a University Student.

Summer is coming to a close and it is time for College to begin. With all personal belongings and supplies ready to go, the freshman student is all set for the first semester to kick off. Things seem to be going well as they get acclimated to campus life and the new surroundings as well as friends. This College Student starts to feel all grown up as they receive their first and second "student" credit card offered to them by the banks.

Throughout their years at university, they are busy as a beaver getting good grades. The studious habits pay off and they graduate with flying colors, perhaps with Honors! Proud of their accomplishment, they want to go off to the work world to pursue work in the field they got a College degree in. A job is secured and they start to create some income. Then, the student loans begin to be due.

College students who choose the full time work path can get a leg up on getting hired at jobs that may be higher than entry level. There is also a chance they may be able to get a higher starting pay too, so they are not necessarily stuck with minimum wage. The other advantage for the College graduate is that they may be considered for management more easily since they have demonstrated an ability to work hard based on the merits of them earning their university degree.

BUT ARE YOU MAKING ANY MONEY

I mentioned earlier in Chapter 1, Part Time Game, that if a college student chooses to work part time while in college, they are not making much money at all. In fact, it becomes a major detraction from their studies.

Now if a College graduate were to pick up Part Time work only, it would fall in the same category as what I mentioned about Minimum Wage jobs. The Part Time job would be a complete waste of their time and they would be struggling to earn enough money to float paying their student loan payments and other financial obligations.

The same College graduate pursuing a full time job will fare much better since they will be earning perhaps 2 times what they could earn via Part Time work. They will have stronger earning ability since corporations favor full time employees for promotions and steady pay raises.

The challenge with College Degrees is that the graduate is buried up to their eyeballs in student loan debt, in most cases, unless they were blessed enough to have full paid scholarships during the college years. So even if they are making really good pay at the full time job, the student loan payments will eat a good amount of their pay over 10 to 25 years afterward.

Keep in mind the following college debts racked up by students according to sites like Forbes, CNN and other financial sites:

1) 2-year colleges can cost $10,000 to $30,000

2) 4-year public colleges can cost $30,000 and up

3) 4-year private colleges can cost $60,000 and up

4) 4-year Ivy League colleges can cost $150,000 to $250,000

The other challenge may be the result of all the credit cards accepted and used during their college years. Most college students are notorious for maxing out all of their credit cards. Then, they are stuck with large monthly payments on the interest of the debt they accrued. The credit card companies make easy money off the hard work of these young financially inexperienced people.

Thus, how much money can a College graduate actually earn and keep if they have this heavy financial baggage from their College years? They have the potential to make as much money as they want, but are continually having to worry about the outgoing expense of this College student loan debt.

CONCLUSION ON COLLEGE DEGREES

College Degree graduates typically have a big financial handicap which is like a thorn on their side. This income path, most often, comes with large lingering education costs. This makes it not the best path to pursue. It is usually one of the more challenging ways to amass large savings. This is why, depending upon the pay received while working full time, the people that never attended college are 1 to 5 years of earnings ahead of College Degree graduates at the onset of getting jobs.

By no means am I downplaying the value of an education, nor the benefit it may have in securing specific careers that may require it as a pre-requisite. However, when we face the facts that as much as 90% of College Degree graduates do not end up in careers related to what they went to school for, it seems like a complete waste of time and money from this point of view. This is especially true when people choose majors like Liberal Arts which is a made up College term where no such related career exists in the real world of jobs.

Grandpa Jesse would smile when people would talk about their College Degrees as a rite of success passage and a guarantee for a high paying career. Gone are the days of companies giving lavish full range benefit packages with beefed up pensions at retirement. With rising inflation also comes the challenge of higher College tuition costs as well. So just like the devaluation of the currency, there is a devaluation of the earning power of the College Degree graduate as they have to repay larger student loan debts.

SOLUTIONS

Unless a College student is pursuing a College Degree for a specific career track which mandates they must attend school at a particular institution, then here is what I personally suggest:

1) Choose a public college for a 4-year college instead of a private college will cut the student loan debts in half.

2) Although Ivy League colleges are viewed as prestigious and elite, there is no sure bet it will secure a high paying job just because it shows up on the resume. If possible, choose a public college for a 4-year college instead of an Ivy League college. Student loan debts will be an average of 15% what would be owed for Ivy League student loan debt.

3) A student may have their heart fixated on going to college, however the person is unsure what career field they want to pursue while in college. They would be much better off going to a 2-year college rather than locking themselves into the 4-year college. This choice alone would give them time to figure out what they want to pursue. More importantly, this will cut the student loan debts in half from what they would pay for a 4-year public college.

4) The best choice of all for clueless, confused or ignorant students who are not sure if they even want to go to college at all, would be to abstain completely. Uncertainty breeds the lack of sound action; thus

the student will be spinning in proverbial circles wasting both their own time and money if they pursued any college classes.

This person can save themselves so much time, pain and a big chunk of money they would have been stuck paying in the form of student loan debt. This person is better off finding full time employment right awaQWA52y or another income path proving worthwhile pay.

3. INTERNSHIPS GAME

People love to gain experience in a field which has been their major study in college. This "in the field" time is helpful to enrich the scope of knowledge for that specific topic. The person gains hands-on real life practice that can assist them is determining if they want to continue down that career path. If the experience is positive, then the individual may seek work in that arena. If it does not turn out so great, the person is able to reflect upon this and make a different choice for future work.

Even if a person has not gone to college for a certain field, some companies may still bring them on as an intern. It is almost like a modern day apprentice program for some corporations. The company wins by finding some talented people to potentially hire. The person wins by learning on the job skills. This individual also is able to take their potential career for a drive to see if it is the right fit.

BUT ARE YOU MAKING ANY MONEY

On the surface, the Internship seems like a really wonderful match made in heaven where both parties, the company and the intern, both get to test each other out without a long term commitment. Definitely seems innocent enough.

The challenge with Internships is that the intern is volunteering their time working for the company for FREE or almost next to FREE. The company does not have to legally treat them as an employee, so if they want to get rid of the intern just because the wind blew the wrong way per se, there is not much recourse an intern would have for being let go. Even paid interns typically receive Minimum Wage, so they will be in the same boat I mentioned before about Minimum Wage earners.

Thus, how much money can an Internship candidate actually earn and keep based on these factors? Most often, not much at all. They only have something to put on their resume or cv (curriculum vitae).

CONCLUSION ON INTERNSHIPS

I do firmly believe that there is a massive value to being on an Internship. It will teach you so much before pursuing a long term career in a specific field. Grandpa Jesse always told me that the people who got paid to do what they love experience heaven on earth. So in essence, if you can land a paid Internship, then even better than a volunteer Internship as you may just be pursuing something which you will love.

Internships have a dark side to them too. Corporations are able to get FREE or very dirt cheap non-employee labor. All of the profits that they can create based upon Intern work is similar to the game that is played in regards to the labor performed by inmates at penitentiaries. In terms of commerce, the corporation is the winner in both Internships and the Jail scenarios. Increased production leading to increased company revenue; all while adding less overhead is always a smile creator for any investor and board of directors.

SOLUTIONS

If a person seeks to be on an Internship, they must protect themselves at all costs. Since Internships are not a great path for wealth creation nor personal income, you should only pursue Internships based on passion for the chosen career. Being honest with one's self about this will make all the difference in how this experience will turn out.

If at all possible, favor a paid internship over a voluntary one. At least you can have some financial compensation for the work you perform for the company regardless of what you choose to do in the future in that field of work. Also, consider heavily the length of time frame the Internship will endure. The longer the Internship goes without worthwhile pay, the more challenging it will make it for you to create lifestyle later on as you may have accrued a certain load of debt while on the Internship.

4. CORPORATE LADDER RESUME CARROT GAME

There is a thrill of starting on the ground floor with a thriving company and growing alongside it. Companies can motivate their employees with the incentive to work hard and get promoted from within. As an employee reaches certain levels of promotion, they reach a cushy management level position and will start receiving special company perks besides their substantial pay increases.

My father, Richard Shamus (picture; mid 1960's), took a different path for his career than his father (my Grandpa Jesse) and paternal grandfather (my Great Grandpa Fishel). There came a day, after graduating high school, that my dad casually picked up a job with a Corporate 100 company. He did not intend to be a career employee and did not know what he wanted to do with his working life yet.

That company held an employee training meeting for all entry level employees. My dad went to this meeting with a neutral mindset and open to hearing what the big shots there had to say. One of the top honchos made a very moving speech near the end of the closing minutes of the event. This gentleman spoke about the virtue of being a company man and the honor it will bring to your family.

My father bought into this philosophy on that day and began his long journey of 40 years there. Dad committed himself to become the very best company man he could be. He offered himself completely to the whims of the company.

Time went by with the company taking notice. My dad rose to new career heights by becoming the Manager of a large territory as a reward for his efforts. As he stayed loyal to the company, he saw increases in pay and of course some recognition at company banquets and such.

Richard Shamus in the 1960'st

BUT ARE YOU MAKING ANY MONEY

There are countless success stories of people that choose the Corporate Ladder path for their career. I'm sure that all of us know at least one person who has done well and moved up the Corporate Ladder.

In terms of the positions being financially rewarding, the answer is both yes and no. Yes, it is very achievable to earn a substantial salary with certain jobs. And No, not every position will pay as lucrative at others.

In terms of saving money and sustaining long term lifestyle… if you can last relatively long at a company and receive good pay, then Yes! On the contrary, hop companies too often or have lower pay scale, then you will be hard pressed for doing so.

The challenges with the Corporate Ladder are:

1) <u>Inflated Job Potential Hype</u>:

The job of the Human Resource department is to not only find the right talent to fit the job, but also to build the candidate's excitement for future possibilities within the company. The advertisements for seeking talent which are placed by the Human Resource department can be laced with exaggerations and in some cases bait-and-switch. A candidate thinks they could be hired for one position, but then is told not even a few days later during the interview the position has already been filled.

As time goes forward, it is not uncommon for many employees' to feel that the experience in their position is not exactly what they were told it would be. The employee feels disillusioned and gains resentment. If by chance that they entered their current position due to a bait-and-switch, the level of anger, frustration and resentment become very high. This is why some people start to look for other work or even "Go Postal".

2) <u>Resume / CV (curriculum vitae) Hype</u>:

Companies do want to hire highly qualified candidates as well as people who may be able to perform well once on the job. So yes, it makes sense to know about the background experience and education of your potential employee candidates. The problem though is that this is not the result that occurs when resumes / cv's (curriculum vitae's) are created and submitted with applications for employment.

Many prospective employees will embellish their background and get creative with past jobs and other experience. I'm not saying that most people will lie when creating their resumes / cv's (curriculum vitae's), but it is apparent that there is some puffery going on. Also, yes there are some people who do make up a colorful past because they really want to wow a company's Human Resource department and hopefully get hired.

The Resume / CV (curriculum vitae) game from the view point of the company does not make sense based on "the rule of future performance". This rule states that past performance does not equal future performance. So just because you were an overachiever in the past in something does not guarantee you will repeat this again. The same is true if you really sucked at something in the past, it does not mean you are stuck as a failure in that forever.

So if companies are ONLY looking to qualify potential candidates based on past performance, they are missing out on some really talented people who may be late bloomers in those skills. But since companies are mainly focused on reducing costs of learning curve training and risk of hiring a low quality performing employee, the Human Resource departments usually bypass "the rule of future performance" and opt to focus mostly on what is in the resume / cv (curriculum vitae).

Although they will have a potential candidate come in for interview(s) with key personnel, this is typically ONLY for the purpose of seeing congruency between what is written in the resume / cv (curriculum vitae) and what they say in person when asked trigger questions. Congruency means that the candidate appears to be genuinely the same in person as what they allege to be on their resume / cv (curriculum vitae).

3) <u>You are Just a Number Syndrome</u>:

Smaller companies, especially Mom & Pop outfits still keep the relationships strong and definitely show appreciation for the individuals working for them. However, the larger the corporation is, the more likely that they will devalue you as the individual and start to view you as easily replaceable, if need be.

This is when the Number Syndrome kicks in. They see you as a computer entry on a screen that can be easily erased whenever you don't help them maintain profitability for the shareholders. The corporation does not care that you have children and a spouse depending upon you to create income. If you don't perform to their every expanding demands, then you are easily disposed of.

4) Your Best is Never Enough Conundrum:

Sales Quotas seem to keep rising quarterly even if you are the all-star employee of the year. The Finish Line keeps on moving further away. The carrot on the stick can never be reached for most. For the gifted few who do touch it for a moment, that brief period of celebration is very short lived. It is ridiculously challenging to find any company that will not play this game of carrot on a fishing line. Again, probably only a small Mom & Pop outfit would respect the individuals enough to not play this game.

5) Time is Your Enemy:

If we were talking about a fine wine or aged cheese, time makes them better and more highly prized. In the Corporate Ladder world, the opposite is true as you become both a liability and a bullseye target.

You are a liability due to diminished returns you may produce for the company as well as technology illiteracy that may come from being stuck in older methods of doing things.

You become a bullseye target for many younger motivated employees and investors. The young employees want your job title and job perks. The investors want to save money by having a younger person take a pay cut to do the same job you have been doing.

6) <u>Investors Determine Your Future Job Security</u>:

Investors do not care about the employees. The only thing that matters is the bottom line. This bottom line is **ROI (Return On Investment); aka Overall Profitability**

The company invests financial resources into human resource talent, product research and development, marketing, real estate development and/or leasing contracts, and so forth. So all the investors want to know is what is going to be their return on this investment. They will tweak whatever necessary to reduce liabilities and increase company profits. If this means laying off employees or reducing payroll or removing perk benefits, then so be it.

7) <u>Promotions are Both Politically Based and Limited</u>:

Merit based promotions sound great at the interview, but once you are on the job, that rhetoric goes out the window immediately. The only way most people get promotions in reality are:

a) Death of employee in wanted position

b) Firing of employee in wanted position

c) Retirement of employee in wanted position

d) Voluntary quitting of employee in wanted position

e) Promotion to higher position of employee in wanted position

f) Lateral transfer to other company position of employee in wanted position

g) Opening of new position that you want

When the promotion does occur, it is not based always on performance of the chosen employee. Similar to high school, the "In Crowd" will rise together. So if a certain employee is well liked, they will gain favor over other much more qualified candidates.

On a seedy note, even though there are sexual harassment policies in place, there are some people in power positions in companies who use sex as a political tool. An example would be the movie Disclosure with Demi Moore. Remember that the employee who is desperate or motivated for promotion that agrees to this act is equally culpable.

Option f (lateral transfer) happens whenever a talented employee leaves the company and they need an equally talented employee from elsewhere in the company to fill their spot. The chance of option g (opening of new position) happening in most cases is slim unless a company is experiencing massive growth. An example would be opening up a new market territory; so a new position is created.

Thus, how much money can people climbing the Corporate Ladder actually earn and keep? Most often, those who make top money are the ones who are willing to play the corporate game of politics. They are also the people who do not get emotionally disturbed when the company breaks many promises or changes the rules often.

In terms of wealth creation, that is possible, however a large majority of employees may not last long enough nowadays at one company. So each time they begin at a new company, it is like they have to go 2 steps back before moving forward again. If a person can stay with the same company long enough, then there are strong chances for wealth creation longer term.

CONCLUSION ON CORPORATE LADDER JOBS

My father remained steadfast loyal to his corporate employer for those dedicated 40 years. But the writing was on the wall in the last year or so with other old timer managers being forced to retire early. 5 years before this happened to my dad, I had a telltale premonition dream one night, where I saw his upper management offering him a bribe based retirement package. This was a dream no one wants to see come true, but it did.

I mentioned this dream at the time to my parents, but they just smiled and dad said that would never happen to him. So in 1998, I was over his house for dinner one night. When my father came home from work, he looked as pale as a ghost. He told me that he remembered the story I told him years earlier about my strange dream. He seemed besides himself when he mentioned that he was not sure how I was able to have that insight.

Then he spoke the unbelievable truth of how his district manager had a meeting with him that very day discussing how the company wanted to offer him a retirement package. The exact words went something like, "if you choose not to accept this package, you may not have a chance again to get this offer".

This is corporate slang for the company finding a reason to release him of employment, one way or another.

Dad ended up taking the retirement package they offered, but many other 55+ year old employees, who had been long term employees and solid managers, did not fare as well. They lost their jobs at some point later on with no special incentive retirement package. They literally were lucky enough to get a pittance of a pension at all based on how many changes the company had gone through in the years preceding the layoffs.

As much as it was a brutal stab in the back, the company would replace these aging loyal managers with young college graduates who were eager to move up the Corporate Ladder. These young new managers received salaries that were less than 65% of what managers like my dad received for the same position.

This is the sad reality of the Corporate Ladder game in action as corporations painfully transition from the Industrial Age to the Information Age. If the Industrial Age had not ended, my father would have served his whole career out at that one company until his natural retirement when he was truly ready to retire. Currently, the Corporate Ladder system really is like the game of chutes and ladders, where your next step could be a chute.

SOLUTIONS

In a post-industrial world, things are not the same as they were even 20 years ago when that world started to crash down. The simple solution years ago during the Industrial Age was to find a stable company that had a good track record in:

1) Industry leader or sharply rising company in their industry

2) Several years of quarterly financial growth

3) Good business reputation

4) Lucrative pension plan

5) Employee friendly policies

6) Low turnover of current employees

7) Strong management grooming program

8) Aggressive employee benefits package

9) Customer service is a top priority instead of profits only

10) Offers quality employee recognition and reward programs

Now that we are in the Information Age, the preceding list of top qualities sought after for choosing Industrial Age companies to work for is literally upside down. Since a company now can do business virtually online, and may not even need a brick and mortar store front, it changes the game of commerce big time.

The same was true in the 1750's when the Agrarian Age ended, the security given from the land owner disappeared and the onset of agriculture technology started displacing it. So if your family prosperity and security came from working the land for the land owner back then, you would need to find new solutions for a new world financial model.

So, similarly people today are finding themselves adjusting to the massive changes brought upon by the Information Age. So what exactly are some of the solutions that one could do to succeed in the current economic model we live in? Here are a few ideas that may help:

1) Become cutting edge by developing literacy in the current technology used by both business and society. This will give you skills to gain more available jobs and hopefully retain your job since you are competent using technology.

2) Seek to be ahead of the curve. Develop technology savvy to lead a trend and not just follow it. The "innovators" and pioneers always make big money in this Information era. This skill will get you past being just another number for a company. The company will see you as a key player since you may be only one of a few people who know how to do that skill. You become the "Go-To" person. This creates long term security as it reduces the replace-ability factor.

3) Learn to harness your attention towards income producing activities. Spend less focus on attention distractors which will overwhelm you and waste your time. Yes, this includes not spending all day surfing on social media sites spying on people to see what is new for them.

4) Learn to be right to the point in conversations. Grab people's attention quickly. There is so much information being thrown at people daily during this Information Age that your message gets lost quick and is less relevant otherwise. People attention span is short, so you must give them a reason to listen to you or you lose their audience.

5) Creativity and conceptualization become your best skills in this age too. Industrial Age employees spent most of their time on busy work. Information Age employees succeed most when they are good at using their right brain to dream up future possibilities and act on creating / implementing them. "Creative problem solving" is the skill I am referring to.

6) Become an information strategist. This is specialized high demand position that is always needed. Technology evolves at an amazing speed, so a person who is well versed in this role will make incredible money that will keep on paying them long term. Let's face it, you would be a helping cog to all people functioning in this Information Age.

7) Become a communications specialist. This is also a very specialized skill that is in high demand during the Information Age. Realize that there are many different methods of communication which people can use. However, all utilize human communication components such as mouth, ears, hands, and eyes.

Companies that thrive today have internet driven businesses with revolutionary products and / or services. They ALL have state of the art communication technology. It is the innovation of communication that expands business during this Information Age. Thus, as a communications specialist, you assist companies in creating more business; thus increased profits.

INDEPENDENT

INCOME PATH

Summary

The quantity of money made from independent income path type of work may create a very sensational lifestyle, but only if you can build it up solid enough. You will cover your basic monthly bills with ease and have the sort of extravagant life that average people could envy.

Where this type of income path falls short is having a successful blueprint to follow. If you do not, you may find a lot of pain and despair. Hopefully, you will be truly blessed and have a Billionaire mentor working closely with you. For most, this is not the case, and challenges must be overcome to develop the skills and knowledge for making this income path work successfully in your favor.

The key in this work is to 1) create leverage platforms including A) SYSTEMS and B) PEER SOCIAL NETWORKS to build your empire from. 2) Use a high amount of earned income to buy assets and then live off of the earning of those assets.

1. COMMISSION ONLY SALES GAME

Commission Only Sales is a magic leveraging income source where a talented sales person can go from having no money in their pocket to being wealthy relatively quickly with the right product or service offering.

BUT ARE YOU MAKING ANY MONEY

Don't get me wrong, I have seen plenty of great sales people who are selling the wrong thing and make peanuts too. Not every person can pick up work in Commission Only Sales and bring home bank. It really does take a special person who has the skills to communicate, lead others, demonstrate features and benefits of offerings (demos), build relationships, develop trust and move the prospect to the action of consuming whatever the offer is.

Commissionable sales and entrepreneurship can be similar in a sense of sales being made. No sales made in either produces the same $0 income results. So a commissioned sales person must focus on being consistent with producing new and repeat sales every chance they get. Sharp, Commission Only Sales people can truly make big bucks once they hone in their skills and become sales pros.

The challenge with Commission Only Sales jobs is that the work is compelled performance based. So even if you have the best product or service ever invented, if you cannot sell it, you will go broke fast. You need to be sharp as a hunting knife, bleed enthusiasm and come across as "the expert" in what you sell.

You need to become a master of tonality and body language even more than the words you speak. People can sense these things and when you got it, you will rock the house and make lots of money. There is no way to fake this. You either got it or you don't!

Thus, how much money can a person working Commission Only Sales jobs actually earn? Well, that truly depends upon you. Do you have what it takes to rise to the top and shatter all sales records or will you get swallowed down the drain with all the other people who can't cope as Commission Only Sales reps. No one else can make it happen for you. You are the show and you are the "NEO" (reference to the Matrix movies) of your own results. Are you going to be the "ONE"?

CONCLUSION ON COMMISSION ONLY SALES JOBS

Commission Only Sales jobs are one of the strongest ways to make large sums of money. Grandpa Jesse used to say that top gun sale people could write their own paycheck per se. On the contrary, stay the heck out of the kitchen if you don't have what it takes, as Commission Only Sales jobs will eat you up for lunch and throw you in the trash. I have personally seen thousands of really amazing talented people that just couldn't hack it as a Commission Only Sales person.

SOLUTIONS

Nothing beats personal development and sales skill training. It is not about how great the company or product/service you sell is. It is all about how great you are at selling both yourself and that product/service. Furthermore, people don't care about you, they only care about their own needs. So the sooner you can learn to broadcast their favorite radio station which is W.I.I.F.M. (What's In It For Me), the easier sales work is going to be for you.

The following will assist your success in Commission Only Sales:

1) Get yourself to day and weekend seminars that are for personal growth.

2) Read as many books as you can on sales and psychology of people.

3) Take time to network with other successful sales people. Learn from them what techniques and strategies will help you be abundantly successful in the field.

4) Watch massive amounts of online videos about sales and the products/services you are selling. You will learn so much from other talented sales people this way. Successful people know that they must duplicate what other successful people already do.

Grandpa Jesse used to advise me to "Pay Attention" which sounds simple, but you would be surprised how many Commission Only Sales people lack this skill. They have no focus and completely miss the important lessons. They are too busy thinking about getting the sale or spending the money they have not made yet.

One simple tidbit can transform the ordinary to extraordinary. It can mean the difference between unimpressive weekly earnings of $300 - $500 to that of a rock star $1,500 - $2,000. Wow, that really is a gigantic distinction of earning potential differential between $20,000 yearly and $90,000 yearly just due to one important lesson learned and applied.

2. ENTREPRENEUR GAME

My Great Grandfather, Fishel Shamus, was a very skilled Master Tailor and Entrepreneur. He came over to the United States from Europe at the turn of the 1900's. Once established here, he sent for his wife and many children to come as well. He arrived in America with next to no money in his pockets (as seen in this picture with his tattered clothing) but possessed top notch skills, ambition and willingness to socially network. He worked hard and smart for a period of many years.

Things clicked well and he financially flourished as a result. Years later, he owned 3 department stores in the North East United States. Great Grandpa Fishel was the father of my Grandpa Jesse. So I'm sure you can figure out that my Grandfather learned a great deal about life and business at an early age being around his super successful entrepreneur father.

Even my Grandpa Jesse was an entrepreneur for many decades of his life too as he owned a thriving Photography Studio. So my choice from a very young age to be an entrepreneur was just in my blood, literally! I never really felt a stronger connection to any other income path. After all, the life of an entrepreneur is quite adventurous and busy. Never a dull moment as there is always something to develop relating to your business.

Great Grandpa Fishel Shamus

BUT ARE YOU MAKING ANY MONEY

I love the entrepreneur life and everyone who knows me would never imagine me in any other work capacity other than it. Yet, I am the first to speak strongly with warnings to people about the turbulent seas of commerce that can hit your "Entrepreneurial Venture Boat" and sink you.

Perilous storms come from all angles and can hit you when you least expect it. You have to become very well versed on many commercial concepts and contract with countless other talented professionals to help guide you on your journey.

Entrepreneurs are not afraid to risk everything which can lead to seriously happy celebratory highs or pity party depressing lows. I am proof of this as I have had some incredible high points in my life where I have gone cruising on luxury yachts when my business ventures were peaking. I have also hit skid row rock bottom where I did not know if I would have any money to buy food for several weeks or even pay my house note.

Being an entrepreneur is not for the faint of heart. You need to have deep convictions and steadfast internal strength. Unlike working for others as an employee, you are the navigator of your own ship and are responsible for so many challenging choices along the way.

You better be self-directed as well as self-motivated. You better learn to love the pain during the process and not just live only for the prize at the end of the road. It is a dangerous road at times that can make you have unsettling nightmares when pressure is high and things are not working out.

I know plenty of entrepreneurs including myself that have failed our way forward after many ventures that did not succeed. This brings me to the point of how entrepreneurs view failure. Employees have been taught in public schooling and even colleges to avoid failure.

That whole consciousness is driven by a grading system that devalues failure and only rewards success. But in the real world of business, entrepreneurs learn early that the only way to win big is to make errors and correct them the next time around. Entrepreneurs progress towards success by making mistakes, learning, growing and creating new more pinpoint choices on their next attempt.

The challenge with being an Entrepreneur is that the work is all dependent on how good you are at developing a stand-alone business without a safety net from other people. If you prefer to work more independently and are motivated to overcome lots of challenges, the entrepreneur life is a great fit for you. If you feel more comfortable just showing up during specific hours and then not having to worry about anything when you are not getting paid to be there, Entrepreneur life is the last thing you want to do.

Thus, how much money can a person working as an Entrepreneur actually earn? Well, similar to Commission Only Sales, that truly depends upon you. Do you have the right stuff… the abilities that will allow you to conquer industries and impact a local, national or international economy? Only YOU will know this answer. All the Risk and all the Reward will go to you. Are you going to be the talk of the town or just another bankrupt company?

CONCLUSION ON ENTREPRENEUR VENTURES

Entrepreneurial Ventures are also on the top of the list for ways to make insane money and get wealthy. Grandpa Jesse thought like an entrepreneur his whole life and that impacted his financial successes.

He always had plenty of liquid cash, even once he chose to be a full time employee later in life. Therefore, life was much more fun for him and my grandmother. Grandpa never stressed about how much things costed at restaurants or anywhere else he spent money, for that matter.

The limits seem to be lifted when you choose to be an entrepreneur. Outside of governmental corporate legalities, you are able to write much of your own rules for how you conduct day to day business. You get to structure your venture however it makes sense for you. You can grow extremely large enterprise as you carve out a legacy for your family. If you believe you can grow your own Entrepreneurial brand, then do it.

SOLUTIONS

Entrepreneurs are not created. They are born that way. A person with the drive to be an Entrepreneur can prepare themselves further to be more likely to succeed. Similar to Commission Only Sales people, Entrepreneurs must steadily work on increasing their personal development. An Entrepreneur can only have as much business prowess as they have ambition and skills. Training is priceless and a must have.

Attending mastermind group think type of events can help immensely. There is a synergy when a group of Entrepreneurs work together. You will find many Entrepreneurs at Chamber of Commerce events for this reason. Also, private groups for the purpose of sharing business ideas is smart practice. This is why there are business unions and / or organizations that get formed to support the Entrepreneurs of specific industries.

3. HOLLYWOOD ACTING CREDITS GAME

Lights, Camera, Action! The glitz and glamour of Hollywood. Oh the thrill of being discovered, becoming famous and getting "Rich". OMG, who doesn't want to be the center of attention and have hundreds of thousands of adoring fans shouting out your name and always wanting to see what you are doing next.

People from all over the world make the daring decision that they too want to be one of the famous "in crowd "celebrities of Hollywood. So they drop whatever they are doing in their life and move out to somewhere near Hollywood, CA with lofty dreams of making it big in the land of the silver screen.

Once here, one quickly discovers that there is a casting process if you want to work in the Hollywood Acting industry. If you are awake enough from your ambitious dreams, you also fathom that developing acting skills may help your chances of getting roles. So off to acting classes one goes.

Other students and acting instructors you meet with tell you that it is best to be a well-rounded actor /actress. They advise you to take dancing classes, voice lessons and even modeling classes, depending upon which type of Hollywood Acting you would like to pursue (theatre, commercials, television, movies, etc.). So without much trepidation, some begin the balance between acting classes and some other training classes.

Prospective actors /actresses have to get pictures taken so they can get their different "looks "captured. So they set up some photo shoot sessions with 1 or more photographers. Head Shots and full body shots are taken and now they are ready to put together their Acting Resume. They use their favorite "money" Head Shot and then put together a list of their credits and acting experiences.

Then, there is the push to go on auditions so you can be discovered and get some parts. You soon realize after doing all of the leg work yourself to find auditions, you may need some representation to assist you. That is when the Agent comes into play. Their job is to help publicize your talents to the casting directors who seek talent.

At this point, it is important to start hanging out in locations that other successful actors / actresses do. The hope is that there will be a magical meetup with a "Star". Maybe the successful Hollywood Acting "Star" will give needed pointers or take a liking to the person. This is the strong belief and a wishful dream.

As this actor /actress starts to be chosen for parts in various productions, there is a continual adjustment to their Acting Resume. The same goes for updating the photographs used, thus repeating the process of having photo shoots to update Head Shots and Full Body Shots.

BUT ARE YOU MAKING ANY MONEY

No one ever tells the aspiring actors /actresses all they need to know to be successful, so it becomes a guessing game at best. The longer they stay in the Hollywood Acting industry pursuing their dream, the more pieces of this puzzle they uncover.

I had never been to California before the age of 27. I too had certain dreams of being successful in the Hollywood Acting industry.

Even though I spent most of my time as an entrepreneur, the whole idea intrigued me. Unlike most aspiring actors /actress who come to Hollywood for the money and fame, I was ONLY seeking the lifestyle.

So I made plans to abandon the current life I was leading including all the friends and family I would very regularly see on a daily or weekly basis. I use the term abandon (yes it is a strong ugly word) since I geographically moved 3,000 miles away from where I called home. I then transplanted myself to a new home with new friends and around a whole different socio-economic environment. Communication with friends and loved ones changes when you live so far away as you don't spend the same quality time with them any longer.

I purchased my plane ticket and was all set for my inspirational journey towards the land of magic. As murphy law would have it, the week I moved to Southern Cal, was the week of 9/11. No one knew what the heck was going on and no one in my circles of influence were going to get on an airplane no matter what, obviously due to the circumstances. Let's face it, there was too much chaos and confusion going on everywhere.

So I opted to drive from upstate NY all the way to Hollywood, CA in my own car. Very ambitious, yet when motivation and dreams are high, there is no price or pain large enough to get in the way. The journey went by fast and I arrived in 3 days. Wow, I was so excited to get here, that I overcame seriously incredible odds and drove more than 1,000 miles a day.

Once I arrived, I needed to get a grip on a few essential things including the first priority; having a place to live. I amazed myself and got that accomplished the day after arriving. Check! Living quarters all set. Now it was time to start meeting up face to face with a few people I had connected with through Craigslist and a few other websites.

Yes, I began going through all of the same type of processes that the Hollywood Acting crowd goes through. I took acting classes, hired an agent, met with dozens of photographers for different picture "looks". I spent my share of time at the "hot spots" where celebrities and successful Hollywood Acting talent go.

I will keep the experiences I had in Hollywood brief as I could write volumes of books just on things I saw, heard and experienced. There truly was that much I took in within the proceeding months after arriving. I will just give you a summary of what I learned.

I am a quick learner and like a chameleon, I am good at adapting to any situation, yet I found the Hollywood industry perplexing and cold. What I found out was Hollywood and the components within it that make it function are all businesses. Their whole business model and modality for generating profits is to get aspiring actors / actresses to subscribe to their thinking process and make money servicing the Hollywood Acting industry.

Hollywood is a business and you become your own franchise. You need to pay for all your own expenses. You need to look the part. You have to pay for your clothing, tanning, professional grooming (hair, pedicures or acrylic nails and makeup) and other image related expenses. You need to pay for a fitness membership so you can get in tip top shape. You need to pay for training classes (acting, modeling, dancing, voice, etc.). You need to pay for photographers. You need to pay for all socially driven activities to be around the lime light "in crowd". You need to pay for Union fees of SAG-AFTRA ("Screen Actors Guild" merged together with the "American Federation of Television and Radio Artists").

All of these expenses add up quick and you better have money coming in and lots of it to cover all of these costs. This is where the majority of aspiring actors / actresses stumble. It is not a little bit of money we are talking about here. Over time, it can add up to many tens of thousands of dollars or more out of your pocket just for the hope and prayer of making it in Hollywood.

Acting Resumes seem no different than Resumes used for jobs until you see how the casting directors will use them as a tool against you. They are a con job at best for most actors / actresses. This is due to the fact that a big percentage of Hollywood Acting projects offer NO PAY, but may give you acting union credits in some cases to get your Union card or keep it.

The level of discrimination and politics that goes on due to the Union of SAG-AFTRA is crazy. For example, actors / actresses who are qualified members of the union may not work for any non-union Hollywood Acting projects. That would keep a SAG- AFTRA Union member barred from performing in many independent projects that the financial powers of the Hollywood Acting industry choose not to support. Thus, they are voting with their influence to block top actors away from being a part of those projects.

Also, if you want any role in Hollywood that actually pays well, you are literally at the mercy of getting SAG-AFTRA qualified. So you go from role to role hoping to get enough Union credits to be able to apply to the Union. Since there are only roughly 160,000 people with SAG-AFTRA membership according to the Union's own website, which means that everyone else is locked out of the big pay day projects until they submit to the requirements of the Union.

So imagine being an actress / actor working hard to audition for roles over and over, hoping to get decent pay. Even if you land a good role in a non-union project, the pay is either low or nothing. They may offer a Union credit or like most productions, offer no credit at all. So the only thing you may use the role for would be your Hollywood Acting reel (video clips of your best work) and to add to your Acting Resume.

Another discrimination seen in Hollywood is the unwritten policy against hiring more women directors. The Hollywood machine does not want women to be in these type of roles. This is a sex discrimination issue. The federal government's EEOC (Equal Employment Opportunity Commission) has been investigating Hollywood for a long about on this problem and even has been contemplating taking legal actions.

So if you are a female considering directing work in Hollywood, at least at the moment, you may find it really difficult to be hired on as such by most studios. You will be forced to take acting roles or other project support work. Your dream to be a director may happen one day, so lots of praying for change is in order.

The challenge with Hollywood Acting is:

1) It is a business disguised as a job. People get confused thinking it is a job since you will be on a payroll of some film studio / company, regardless if they are independent or not. However, the industry is called "Show Business" The reason for this is 2 fold.

    a) No Show, No Business.

    b) Hollywood Acting is a Business, not a job for you.

2) You must pay for every expense yourself until you are blessed enough to break through the glass ceiling and become one of the successful ones that "made it"

3) Acting Resumes indirectly force an actor /actress to support the acting union plus diminish the value of their own acting efforts in the process. There is a need to "Pay Your Dues" they are told.

4) Success in Hollywood comes with a price on your privacy. Once you cross the threshold and start to do well, you begin to lose your private life as paparazzi follow you and take pictures and videos of you everywhere. It is hard to truly "get away" from it.

5) Tons of Hollywood industry related businesses take advantage of aspiring actors / actresses by offering overpriced services that are either needed or more often never needed. There is no protection for the novice and since the veteran actors / actresses know better, they usually don't get burned by much of this pillaging.

6) If you are an Ethnic Minority like Asian, Indian or Arab, for instance, you have a much more difficult time finding good paying projects. The stereotypes built up for these groups are both outdated and insulting. Asians are segmented usually into martial art type of movies. Bollywood was started due to the unfair treatment that Indians received in Hollywood. Africans in Nigeria created Nollywood, again for the same reason. Most importantly, if these Ethnic Minorities do get a decent role, it is typically not the lead role in the project.

7) The casting couch is alive and well. Sex is one of the dirty underbellies of the industry. So many people who have a genuine shot at making it big in Hollywood go through this ritual per se, whereby some big shot producer or director will sexually proposition the aspiring actor /actress.

If the sexual advance is not accepted, the actor / actress does not get the role or the green light to become a bigger star. However, should the actor / actress accept the nasty advance of this sleazy sexual predator, there is strong chance for getting a certain upcoming role or a true shot to be in the Hollywood limelight with big name acting super stars.

Thus, how much money can people choosing to pursue Hollywood Acting actually earn and keep? It is going to depend upon whether or not one becomes a "working" actor. If so, they can make a living if they can secure steady work. If not, it is not likely at all. Much of the available statistics do not take into consideration the part time non-working actors / actresses who may land a few acting projects from time to time.

The following statistic chart come from the National Endowment for Arts for the years 2006 through 2010. From all the data gathered and results provided, it appears the stats derive from full time working actors/ actresses.

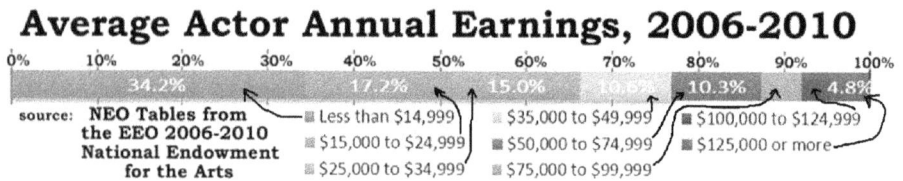

Average Actor Annual Earnings, 2006-2010

0%	10%	20%	30%	40%	50%	60%	70%	80%	90%	100%
34.2%			17.2%		15.0%		10.6%	10.3%		4.8%

source: NEO Tables from the EEO 2006-2010 National Endowment for the Arts

- Less than $14,999
- $15,000 to $24,999
- $25,000 to $34,999
- $35,000 to $49,999
- $50,000 to $74,999
- $75,000 to $99,999
- $100,000 to $124,999
- $125,000 or more

What is very transparent from these reported results is:

1) 77% earned less than $50,000 per year which would be less than $961 per week.

2) 66.4% earned less than $35,000 per year which would be less than $673 per week.

3) 51.4% earned less than $25,000 per year which would be less than $481 per week.

4) 34.2% earned less than $15,000 per year which would be less than $288 per week.

So what exactly does this mean? It means that full time working actors fared no better off than Corporate Ladder full time employees, since according to the Bureau of Economic Analysis the statistics mirrored the same percentages and earnings. But the statistical data from the Bureau of Economic Analysis had 1 HUGE difference.

Actor Age Demographics, 2006-2010

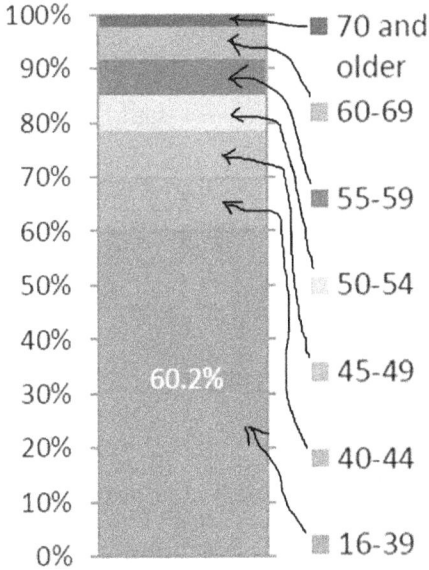

Chart showing stacked bar of actor age demographics with percentages from 0% to 100%. Categories: 70 and older, 60-69, 55-59, 50-54, 45-49, 40-44, 16-39. The 16-39 segment shows 60.2%.

source:

NEO Tables from the EEO 2006-2010

National Endowment for the Arts

Take a look at the preceding Actor Age Demographics chart. This is also from the National Endowment for Arts for the years 2006 through 2010. This is mind blowing! It literally shows that if you are an actor over the age of 50, you have less than 20% chance of making any real money in Hollywood.

This means that Hollywood gives casting preferential to younger actors/actresses and discriminates against those past a certain age. The chart clearly shows proof that 3 out of every 5 paid full time workers in the Hollywood industry are between the ages of 16 and 39. Thus, if you are in that young age group, you can earn a substantial income.

But be cautious, because one would have a very limited amount of finite time to break the glass ceiling and become a super star actor /actress before Hollywood will block your path towards this. This means that a young actor / actress must do all they can during those years to "make it" big or else watch their career fade away.

With this type of monetary reality, it is clear to see why Acting is great as a job and will pay the bills. However, with less than 8% of full time working actors being able to earning more than $100,000 per year, it is not a great vehicle to pursue if you want to guarantee making big money.

CONCLUSION ON HOLLYWOOD ACTING

As entertaining as Hollywood Acting can be, choosing to make money in this field is a tough proposition. Granted, there are the visible celebrities who may earn top pay. These elite 4.8% who earn more than $125,000 per year, should never be seen as a blanket financial reality for most who work in Hollywood.

Residual Royalty payments from acting projects is where the long term retirement type of money can start to be built. Whenever there is a Royalty financial agreement given to an actor /actress, they will receive ongoing payments anytime there is monetary compensations coming in from the project based on their specific Royalty contract details.

Know that there is a large amount of people who are not seen in front of the camera who support all the visible movie stars. These people have good pay coming in when they have film projects, but it is never a big pay day unless they are the producer or director for a decent budget production.

SOLUTIONS

If a person has their heart firmly set on making it big in Hollywood Acting or go bust, there are a few recommendations I have that may assist them. These are only my opinions, yet I soundly believe, if applied, these ideas with increase the odds of that person being one of the few who become part of that magic story of Hollywood; thus, the stuff that legends are built from.

1) Embrace who you are. Get used to rejection and do not listen to criticism when going on auditions. Everyone has an opinion and the only opinion that matters is yours. Listen to your heart and be yourself no matter what. Do not change for anyone and don't take crap from anyone either. This includes casting directors saying you are too fat, too tall, your hair is too curly, too serious, too ugly, too nerdy, etc.

2) Forget perfection. It will ruin your Hollywood dream. Aim high and work hard. Work ethic trumps talent or experience.

3) Extrude confidence. Hollywood is the valley of ego. Low self-esteem and shy personalities do not do well in Tinsel town.

4) It's NOT "WHAT" you know in Hollywood, It's "WHO" you know. So become good at Networking and leveraging your connections.

5) Work for a Casting Agency. This is cool because you will hear about projects available and may even start to land small parts sporadically as a result.

6) Become a PA (Production Assistant) first to learn the film making process and develop incredible contacts along the way. You can always get in front of the camera later on when the time is right. Be careful though, as there are.

7) Thousands of PA's. Competition will be fierce, but well worth it when you can make this PA strategy work for you.

8) Become an assistant to an Actor / Actress, Producer or Director who has already made it. Yes, you may be performing menial tasks like getting their coffee, meals or doing their dry cleaning. The positive side of things is that you may get to be on sets with them and meet other movers and shakers in Hollywood.

9) Work in the Mail Room for a Talent Agency. You will gain invaluable insights into how the deals are made and you just never know what you will come across.

10) Find a peer group to support each other's dreams of making it big in Hollywood. Like some of the other Click's everyone has seen in the industry like the Brat Pack in the 1980's, Hollywood

Acting colleagues help each other get roles in projects when one of them gets a foot in the door.

11) Get yourself on the internet and pimp yourself out. YouTube, Facebook, Instagram and other social media do work. There have been big celebrities that were found this way. You could be next.

12) Los Angeles is not the ONLY place for Acting. There is also New York, NY; Atlanta, Georgia; Orlando, Florida and several others acting hub locations in the USA.

4. NETWORK MARKETING GAME

Work from Home is a very appealing concept and people from all walks of life seem to have done this at some segment of their life. More recently, this trend has become ever more popular as technology becomes more advanced, yet easier to use and the economy continues on a depression level decline. For those wanting the freedom to work on their own schedule where ever they have a phone and internet connection, this is a great solution.

The hook is, that Network Marketing is a poor man's franchise system whereby for usually under $1,000 you can buy into that franchise and get enough marketing tools, product supplies and training to be in business. The beauty of the system is that the company has already spent their resources on developing all the products/services you will offer and the marketing tools needed to sell them.

BUT ARE YOU MAKING ANY MONEY

The challenge with Network Marketing is that a large majority of people that choose to join this field do not have:

1) The background as a business owner

2) Self-directed discipline to independently be successful

3) Monetary backing to invest in marketing and business operating expenses

4) Communication skills to effectively talk with people

5) A High level of self-esteem to believe enough in themselves that they can do it

6) Thick rhino skin to take massive levels of rejection

7) Long term thinking to weather the storm of challenges faced during the formulation phase of your personal business

8) Influence over other movers and shakers who can grow business quickly due to their know how and connections

9) Sales skills to retail products to cash flow the business and to create strong residual stream from long term personal customers

10) Willingness to be coachable and learn new strategies that work in the Network Marketing Industry

11) Engagement in income producing activities that create results

12) Support system of other highly successful people in Network Marketing

The folks who join a Network Marketing company may not possess some or all of the preceding traits. Many of these people, if they do not receive the attention needed to correct this or are not willing to have the personal development to grow into these skills, will come to a brick road at some point, get frustrated and quite angry. These are the folks that regularly leave the Network Marketing industry.

Thus, how much money can a person without the proper traits and skills have in Network Marketing? I know that we both know the answer is very little, since statistically more than 80% of promoters in the industry produced not even enough income every month to pay for their ongoing monthly business operating expenses.

Another 10% made just a few hundred dollars at best in profits. It is the remaining 10% that are the successful ones which people tell the stories about. Be mindful that only the top 5% are making the big money while everyone else is dreaming big but falling short of achievement of that vision.

CONCLUSION ON NETWORK MARKETING

I know from personal experience of 23 years of being a promoter myself, that there are many people who do have success in Network Marketing and can make it work for them. In fact, during several of those years via my own involvement, I was one of those top 10% people who was making money and achieving success.

However, the only way it can work, in my opinion, is a person has got to have a rock solid mentor, have a very large ongoing budget to invest into growing their business and be willing to fill their calendar up with face to face meetings. Network Marketing is not going to work very well for those who lack money, hustle or influential connections.

SOLUTIONS

Network Marketing affords the special few 10% an amazing recurring income and high quality lifestyle when they can get to this level of achievement. It is not a simple pay to play lottery model where a person pays a large franchise sum to join a company and hit it big overnight to become stinking wealthy. There is a lot of personal development that is needed as well as a decent amount of personal resources.

Similarly, a person wanting success in this industry should not just wait for their "upline" or "company" to perform magic to part the red sea or raise the dead and build their business for them. It requires a die-hard commitment and unwavering focus on building your business night and day, just like any other entrepreneur might do.

To win in this profession:

1) Never miss company held events

2) Plug into all the training you can

3) Communicate daily with upline team members

4) Seek support constantly

5) Keep growing your own skill sets so you will become sharper and more refined by the day.

6) Develop new relationships daily to increase your social circle and become a master of influencing others. People tend to be followers towards those they view as more successful than themselves.

CLOSING

Whew! That was a mouthful. That is how some of you might feel every day as you struggle to get more income coming in to support the lifestyle dream you aspire to create. Don't fret my friends. There is no need to feel overwhelmed. I know from being down all these paths that they don't have to stop you from the life you are ready to live.

Don't just close this book and smile, thinking that you just entertained yourself with an enjoyable read. Do something about your situation to positively affect your monetary position. Create the segway to your fiscal victory to break your struggle once and for all. A little bit of belief, some proper planning and taking a step forward will set you in motion.

Go after your dreams. Work smart and put in the effort needed to be fruitful. Most importantly, any time you find yourself struggling to make finances come together for your future. Please feel free to borrow the strong guiding voice of my grandpa. Hear the words as they progressively keep chiming in your head over and over until you find the answer you seek. I know the answer is close at hand.

"But Are You Making Any Money?"

"But Are You Making Any Money?"

"But Are You Making Any Money?"

"But Are You Making Any Money?"

Thank You!

Marc Shamus

ABOUT THE AUTHOR

Marc Shamus is a teacher of life strategies and ideas that may improve the quality of the people's lives. He is a Published Author, Life Educator, Public Speaker and Entrepreneur.

Learn more about Marc at:

iMasterLife.com/MarcShamus

Learn more about Marc's Publishing Company at:

iMasterLife.com

PERSONAL DEDICATION

This book is very personal to me. I want to give the deepest appreciation to all the people who influenced me in my life. You **ALL**, in some special way, assisted in my gaining the wisdom and experiences in life to write this book.

To my smart, gifted, gorgeous and funny children; you pick me up when I am down, you make me smile when I need a laugh, you give me energy when I am tired, you Love me with all of your hearts and I am forever humbled and speechless. "I LOVE YOU!"

Kimiko Shamus, Kuki Shamus, Zen Shamus, Kali Shamus & Zivena Shamus

To my Mom & Dad (Phyllis & Richard Shamus); you have always been my biggest fans since day 1, I want to shout from the roof tops that "I LOVE YOU!"

Phyllis & Richard Shamus

To my brother Arnie Shamus; you always saw the silver lining in every cloud and would remind me of that at times I was focused on the rain. "I LOVE YOU G!" – (J & J All the Way)

Arnold Shamus (Right) And I (Left)

To the great memories of my 4 Grandparents (Harold Mickelson, Eva Mickelson, Margaret Shamus & Jesse Shamus) you taught me to love unconditionally, to edify those you love, how life can be "very good", how to see the beauty in all of Mother Nature, and the value of working wise to develop wealth. "I LOVE YOU!"

Eva & Harold Mickelson

Margaret & Jesse Shamus

Did You Love But Are You Making Any Money?

Thank you for investing in yourself and in this book.

If you enjoyed this book, please let others know how much they can benefit from it by leaving a review here:

iMasterLife.com/Reviews/Shamus

If you have feedback on how to make this book even better, I'd love to hear it at **info@imasterlife.com**

Thanks!

Marc Shamus

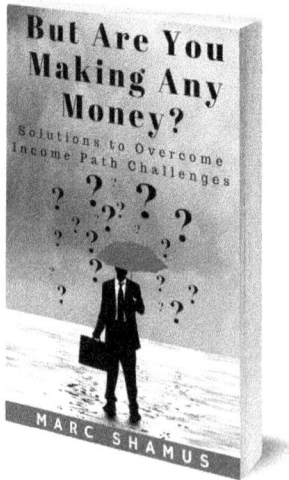

Thanks again for your support!

RECOMMENDED PUBLICATIONS

Go to:

iMasterLife.com/develop

WATCH OUR VIDEO COURSES

Get access to training video courses by going to

iMasterLife.com/Courses

Inside these course, you'll discover...

• What are the <u>Basics</u> of each taught subject

• How to <u>Make</u> <u>Your</u> <u>Life</u> <u>Better</u> as you learn & apply lessons

• How <u>Powerful</u> "YOU" really are

iMasterLife.com/Courses

INCOME PATHS & SOLUTIONS WORKSHEETS

What type of income paths have you tried and what solutions did you use? Jot down all ways you worked to create money. Then remember what you did, if anything at all to solve the gap that income path created.

Income Path #1

Solutions to Income Path #1

1)

---

2)

---

3)

---

4)

---

5)

Income Path #2

Solutions to Income Path #2

1)

_____

2)

_____

3)

_____

4)

_____

5)

Income Path #3

Solutions to Income Path #3

1)

---

2)

---

3)

---

4)

---

5)

Income Path #4

Solutions to Income Path #4

1)

---

2)

---

3)

---

4)

---

5)

Income Path #5

Solutions to Income Path #5

1)

2)

3)

4)

5)

Income Path #6

Solutions to Income Path #6

1)

---

2)

---

3)

---

4)

---

5)

Income Path #7

Solutions to Income Path #7

1)

_____

2)

_____

3)

_____

4)

_____

5)

Income Path #8

Solutions to Income Path #8

1)

---

2)

---

3)

---

4)

---

5)

Income Path #9

Solutions to Income Path #9

1)

2)

3)

4)

5)

Income Path #10

Solutions to Income Path #10

1)

2)

3)

4)

5)

www.ingramcontent.com/pod-product-compliance
Lightning Source LLC
Chambersburg PA
CBHW060625210326
41520CB00010B/1474